# FORWARD

I am delighted that Duane Sparks chose to write a book that shows so clearly and dramatically how vital questioning skills are to a salesperson—especially when those skills are applied within the broader framework of the Action Selling system.

CARQUEST began teaching Action Selling to our 1,200 outside salespeople in 2005, in connection with a corporate initiative that our CEO calls the Journey to the Elite. The Journey has to do with transforming CARQUEST from a good company to a great one. The phenomenal results we have achieved with Action Selling are due to what is now an Elite sales force.

Many of our salespeople have been in the field for more than 20 years. When they were merely good, they thought their job was to sell auto parts. To become Elite they had to learn that customers must be sold on all elements of the buying decision, beginning with whether to "buy" the salesperson. They didn't know how or when to "sell themselves" as trusted business consultants. They didn't know that asking—not telling—is the way to make that first and most crucial "sale." Now they do.

Our most experienced salespeople are often the ones with the greatest appreciation for the difference Action Selling makes. Take this example from a veteran CARQUEST sales rep. A week after completing the course, he sent an awed email to his sales manager. "Over my 40-year working career I have taken many, many courses," he wrote. "But let me tell you, this is the first one that truly delivers immediate results. I have been astonished this week at how fast I got results!"

The rep cited six significant pieces of new business he picked up in that first week—mainly by asking more and better questions than he ever had before. His story is no longer unusual at CARQUEST. Reps like this have become Elite because they now understand what you will learn in this book: Why to ask, what to ask, when to ask, and how to ask questions that truly do become The Answer to Sales.


Bob Ring
Dean, College of Sales Excellence
CARQUEST University

# Introduction

*All talk, no sale*

The basic philosophy espoused in this book—that questioning and listening skills, not the gift of gab, are the key to successful selling—is one I have held for years. But the catalyst that finally inspired me to start writing was an encounter with a salesperson who was one of the best gabbers I ever met.

During a recent visit to Hawaii, the food-and-beverage manager of our country club on the Big Island invited my wife and me, together with a group of friends, to a wine-tasting event. The evening featured a presentation by a wine expert who sold high-end vintages to bars and restaurants. The club manager's agenda was to find out which wines we particularly liked so that he could order cases of the stuff; if we bought it, so might his other customers. He promised that we would enjoy the speaker. "The man's expertise is incredible," he said.

Was it ever! The presentation was superb. The speaker was flamboyant, fun, and fascinating. He wowed us with colorful details about the history of wine, how wine is made, how vineyards operate, who were the powers behind particular vineyards—there was no end to his knowledge and no limit to his enthusiasm for the subject. For nearly an hour he held us spellbound.

"Wow," said one of my friends when the evening ended, "that guy is the ultimate salesperson."

I had enjoyed the presentation as much as anyone, but that stopped me. *No*, I thought, *he's the ultimate example of the guy most salespeople think they want to be.*

Terrific though the speaker had been, there was one small problem. Nobody in our group, including the food and beverage manager, bought any wine. And I was confident that I knew why. It was because none of the salesperson's formidable expertise was ever brought to bear on the concerns of any individual buyer. He seemed to know everything there was to know about wine, and he was wonderful at talking about it. But what he *didn't* know was the factors that might have spurred any one of us to open a wallet and buy a case or even a bottle. He didn't know that because he didn't ask. Nor did he invite us to ask questions that might have given him a clue.

My wife, for instance, prefers a good merlot. I'm sure he'd have been able to tell her plenty, but she never got a chance to ask. The guy was absolutely world class at what he did. But what he did was talking. It wasn't selling. As a public speaker, he might have a bright future. As a salesperson, he is a dinosaur. Unless he can adapt and change, I suspect he is doomed. And change will be difficult for him precisely because he is so great at talking—and he enjoys it so.

## What do buyers care about?

If you take nothing else away from this book, for the sake of your career remember this: Three-quarters of the real "selling" that occurs in any sales transaction takes place while the salesperson is listening, not talking. Listening to what? To the customer's answers to careful, thoughtful, open-ended questions about needs and concerns—questions that can't be answered with a simple yes or no and that encourage customers to think and talk about what's important to *them*, not just to the salesperson.

Years of research by The Sales Board show that:

- 95% of customers say that salespeople talk too much.

- On average, successful sales calls include 25% more open-ended questions than close-ended ones. (Conversely, failed calls have 86% more close-ended questions than open-ended ones.)

- The success rate of sales calls rises significantly when more than two specific customer needs are uncovered by questioning. In other words, if a salesperson's questions lead a customer to identify at least three needs relevant to a product or service, the chances of closing a sale increase dramatically.

In truth, successful selling always has had more to do with asking than telling. That fact has been obscured, however, because in years past salespeople could coast further on the gift of gab, coupled with their own knowledge and expertise. In today's world, many customers have as much expertise as the salesperson. And they can easily find out more than they ever wanted to know about a subject just by jumping on the Internet.

This means that the days of the salesperson as a fount of specialized knowledge are over. Where once it was hard to verify or argue with a salesperson's claims, now it is easy. In addition, competition has intensified, and almost all products and services have become commodities. If you are like most salespeople, there is probably little objective difference between your wares and your competitors'. Every day it gets harder to differentiate your product—and especially to justify a higher price—in the classic way, by enumerating "unique" features and benefits.

Knowledge, expertise, and enthusiasm are still important—even vital—for salespeople. But in the battle for customer commitment, the rules have changed. The challenge today is not to "educate" customers by dumping your general knowledge on them. Rather, it is to figure out how to *apply* your expertise to the customer's individual situation. That's what wins hearts and minds—and opens wallets. There may be nothing unique about your product or service, or even about a customer's needs. But what is unique, always, is the customer's perception of his own situation—the reasons why certain needs keep *this* person up at night. The only way to discover those is to get the customer to tell you about them.

To do that, you have to ask good questions. And you have to listen carefully to the answers. By doing so, you earn the customer's permission to ask even better questions. Before you can *talk* about your products in a way that really matters to a potential buyer, you have a lot of listening to do.

## First, sell yourself

How long must you listen before you can start selling? Wrong question. Here's something most salespeople don't understand: As long as you're asking questions and listening carefully to the answers, you *are* selling. You're selling *yourself* to the customer as a potential ally who cares about his problems and wants to help solve them. That's not just incidental to selling your product, it is your Number 1 task. Because customers will not buy your product until they first have bought you.

This is no casual claim. Research has proven that in the course of any major sale, customers make five key buying decisions, and they always make them in a particular order. The first of those decisions is whether to "buy" the salesperson. Before customers will decide to buy your product, before they will settle on your company, and before they decide whether to pay your price, they first must buy you—meaning that they must like *you*, trust *you*, and want to do business with *you*.

Whether to buy the salesperson is not only the first major decision the customer makes but also the most important one. There are two reasons. First, if products cannot be differentiated from competitive offerings based on features and benefits, then the only meaningful differentiating factor is the salesperson. Secondly, if you can establish a relationship in which you are a trusted consultant, ally, and problem solver—someone who understands the client's situation thoroughly—then you will form a lasting bond with the customer. That bond will be difficult for competitors to break.

# The Sales Dinosaur Model

| Cause | Symptom | Consequences |
|---|---|---|
| Failure to Ask/Listen | The inability to:<br>• Get to decision-makers<br>• Win when competition exists<br>• Create urgency<br>• Demonstrate value<br>• Differentiate the salesperson<br>• Differentiate the company<br>• Differentiate the product<br>• Manage (shorten) sell cycles<br>• Keep current customers<br>• Add new customers<br>• Build trust/credibility<br>• Get your price<br>• Prioritize accounts<br>• Handle objections<br>• Present solutions<br>• Gain lasting commitments<br>• Sell solutions vs. transactions | Lost sales<br>Poor margins<br>Unprofessional image<br>Fragile customer relationships |

**Conclusion: Salespeople who lack a plan to improve Questioning/Listening skills are at high risk for extinction.**

### Shut up and sell something

Most of the recurring problems salespeople wrestle with, and most of the excuses they make for lost sales, result from a single cause. It isn't laziness, it isn't a lack of product knowledge, and it isn't that they aren't glib enough. It's that they fail to ask the right open-ended questions and listen to the answers.

Look at the "symptoms" column on the Sales Dinosaur Model. Do you have trouble differentiating your products? Justifying your price? Getting through to final decision-makers? Handling objections? The problem is not that you aren't saying the right things. The problem is that you aren't asking the right questions. Forget about talking your way in to see the ultimate decision-maker. Try *asking* your way up the decision chain until somebody *wants* you to see the big boss. Forget about refining the PowerPoint slides in your product presentation. No matter how pretty they are, until you've asked the right questions, you don't *have* a winning presentation. All you've got is a colorful data dump.

I want to persuade you that successful selling is primarily a matter of asking, not telling. I want to persuade you that if you approach selling that way, a new and better world can open to you. But how can I show you what that world looks and feels like?

As in my previous books, I've tried to do it by telling you a story. This one is about two fellows named Mitch and Harry. They're both great talkers—likeable salespeople with the classic gift of gab. But gab isn't cutting it anymore. One of these guys already knows about the new world I mentioned—the one that begins to open when you learn and use a system called Action Selling. The other is about to discover it. He'll be very glad he did. I think you will be too.

Any questions?

Duane Sparks
Chairman
The Sales Board, Inc.

# CONTENTS

# PREFACE

*'Why can't I compete anymore?'*

itch's drive off the second tee was pretty good, a slight fade landing nicely in the fairway. Harry wondered when Mitch would get around to telling him the real reason why they were on the course this morning.

The call had come a week before, Mitch phoning out of the blue to invite Harry to play a round of golf. "I have an ulterior motive," Mitch had said. "I want to talk to you about a career issue I've got."

Though they spoke on the phone from time to time, they hadn't seen each other for almost four years. Now Mitch had something on his mind. But what? The conversation so far had been limited to catching up on wives, kids and current events. Mitch was fun to be with, as always—outgoing, upbeat, confident. But now the cheerfulness felt a little forced, and the confidence seemed brittle, as if it would shatter if he weren't careful. That was new. So were the worry lines around his eyes.

*You've been under some stress, buddy,* Harry thought. *Why don't you tell me what this is about?*

Harry's drive was a good 20 yards beyond Mitch's. As they began to walk up the fairway, Mitch finally came to the point.

"Bet you're wondering about the career problem I mentioned," he said.

"*That* bet you might win," Harry said, hinting that Mitch wouldn't win their golf bet after his double bogey on the first hole. "What's up?"

The mask of cheerfulness dissolved altogether as Mitch trudged

> ***"I'm losing it. I can't sell anymore."***

across the grass, suddenly oblivious to the beautifully conditioned golf course and the clear, sunny morning. "I'm losing it, Harry," he said. "I can't sell anymore."

"Ah," Harry said when it became clear that Mitch was waiting for a response. "I get it. So you're training to go on the Champion's Tour."

"I'm serious," Mitch said. "Ever since you showed me the ropes back at Walco, when I started out, I've been a top salesperson—number one at three different companies. Or, rather, I was for, what, 12 years? But about two years ago, I started to slip. Lately it's gotten worse—a lot worse. And I don't know why! I'm *good*, Harry, you know I am. But now it ain't working. I'm only 40 years old! I'm too young to be losing my grip."

They reached their balls, dropped their bags, selected clubs, hit their next shots, and moved on. The conversation continued as they played, with breaks dictated by the requirements of a game that was no longer either man's main concern.

"Harry, you're the best salesperson I ever knew," Mitch resumed. "You were my mentor and my role model. The most important things I ever learned about selling, I learned from you. You helped me become successful. And you're still at the top of your game. I did some checking, and I know you're a sales star at your new company. I want to ask you to help me figure out why I'm sliding."

> *"The most important things I ever learned about selling, I learned from you."*

Mitch's words hit Harry like a shanked five iron. *The most important things you've learned about selling*, he thought, *came from the drivel I was spouting back then? I'm sorry to hear that, Mitch. I'm truly sorry.*

"Whoa, slow down," Harry said aloud. "What do you mean by 'I'm sliding' and 'it ain't working'? Give me some specifics."

"Sure," Mitch said bitterly. "Specifically, I was the top sales performer at every company I've been with since you left Walco. I got my current job five years ago and became the top performer there. But two years ago, for the first time since you took me under your wing, I missed my quota. I hit only 82 percent. Last year I hit 74 percent. Now I'm standing at 48 percent of year-to-date quota with just three months left in the fiscal year. Harry, four years ago I hit 140 percent and considered that unremarkable—for me.

"Want more specifics? Last week my sales manager actually called me on the carpet to discuss what she called 'the erosion' in my territory. And she was right. I haven't added a new account in 18 months. Me, Mr. Charm-the-Birds-Out-of-the-Trees! I used to rain new accounts! Not a single new account in a year and a half."

> ### *"My sales manager called me to discuss 'the erosion' in my territory."*

Harry flashed back to a scene of Mitch as a rookie, coming to Harry for approval after landing his first blockbuster account. "Mr. Charm-the-Birds-Out-of-the-Trees!" Harry had exclaimed, giving Mitch a high five. He winced at the memory. He still stuck his wedge shot near the pin, though.

"Why aren't you landing new accounts?" Harry asked. "At what point in the sales process do things break down?"

"Well, for one thing, I'm having trouble getting to decision makers," Mitch said. "I get bogged down with lower-level managers and sometimes even technical specialists. So no matter how great my presentation is, I'm not delivering it to someone with final buying authority."

> ### *"I'm having trouble getting to decision makers."*

*There's more to this than I'm hearing*, Harry thought, as he marked his birdie on the scorecard.

"You're down two," he said. "What else?"

"I don't know," Mitch said, shaking his head, "it just seems there's no urgency to *act* anymore. Everybody's kind of interested, everybody's thinking about making a buying decision—but they want to go on thinking about it forever. The decision-making process drags on, and on, and finally it just kind of peters out."

"Is that always true?" Harry asked. "Or do they eventually decide to buy from someone else?"

"Yeah, I guess a lot of them do," Mitch admitted. "Usually, after all the stalling and so-called agonizing, they just buy on price from the lowest bidder."

"Why would they stall if they're going to buy from the lowest bidder anyhow?" Harry asked.

> *"After all the stalling, they just buy on price from the lowest bidder."*

Mitch flinched as if the question were painful as he sliced his tee ball into the woods. "Once in a while, they go with a competitor who charges more than we do," he said. "Those are the losses that really haunt me. Our product and service package is at least as good as any in the industry. We're a top-of-the-line outfit with a great reputation. I hate to say it, but there's only one reason a customer would pay as much or more for any of our competitors' products, and that's if one of their salespeople just plain outsold me. But I don't know how they do it!"

*I could tell you in three words*, Harry thought, *but you're not ready yet*. He mulled a response while he pulled a six iron for his next shot. Then he said, "Let me see if I've got this straight. You're having serious trouble adding new accounts. You often can't get through to decision makers, and you can't seem to generate any urgency with the people you do see. The buying-decision process either stalls or they buy from someone else—usually, but not always, based on price alone. Does that sound right?"

"Pretty much," Mitch said.

"So, these problems are with new accounts. What's happening with your current clients?"

"That picture's not so hot either," Mitch conceded. "At two large accounts, where I was their so-called 'first call,' I'm now number two or three. The competition is chipping away the mid-market, too, despite the great relationships I have with my clients. Again, I think it's usually price. When it *isn't* price…well, sometimes I hear, 'I didn't know you carried that product.'"

Mitch missed his first putt, jabbed at the second one and then picked up, down three after three holes.

*Are you listening to yourself?* Harry thought. *Those don't sound like "great relationships."* "I see," he said, as they walked to the next tee. "What have you done to try to turn things around?"

"I've tried everything! I've tried more small talk to build better rapport, but everybody's so busy that no one has time to talk anymore. It's just, 'Get to the point.' So I've practiced my delivery in a dozen ways. I've customized my presentation—taken some material from the marketing department and made my own PowerPoint slides that really zero in on our key differentiating points. I'm convinced I have a better presentation than any salesperson in the company. And Harry, you know that when I get going, there aren't many better. I'm stumped."

Harry sighed, as they waited for the group in front of them to clear the green. *Might as well get to it*. "Mitch, do you want to hear it straight?"

"Absolutely. Please."

> *"Everybody's so busy that no one has time to talk anymore."*

"All right then, I have two thoughts. First, you said nobody has time to talk anymore. It would be more accurate to say that nobody has time to listen to *you* talk. Second, whether you designed your presentation or the marketing department did, it doesn't include any differentiating points at all. Because you deliver it before you have any idea what a differentiated need *is*."

Mitch stopped cleaning the grooves of his four iron with a tee. "What do you mean?"

> *"Nobody has time to listen to you talk."*

"First, tell me this: You said the most important things you know about selling came from me. What, exactly, did you learn from me 15 years ago?" Harry braced himself as if he were about to take a beating.

"Are you kidding?" Mitch said. "I remember your favorite line: 'It's not what you say, it's how you say it.' You taught me that everything really important in sales starts with that. It's all about enthusiasm during the pitch. If I act excited, the customer gets excited. With some charisma, I pitch my products confidently and convincingly. I gain credibility. If the customer finds me likeable and credible, then I've won their trust. 'And a customer who trusts you will buy from you,' you always said. You showed me some good techniques, too, but in the end, you said, it comes down to enthusiasm, credibility and trust. And to get those things, it's not what you say; it's how you say it.

"That's what you taught me, Harry, and I know it's true," Mitch continued. "So how come I can't seem to say it right anymore? Sure, people are busier, but has there been some other earth-shaking change I missed? Do they want to hear something different? Or is it me?

"Do I stink?" he asked, sniffing his golf shirt. "Have I grown a giant wart on my nose that's visible to everyone but me? What the heck is going on, Harry? My career is going down the tube."

Harry felt ill. *Yep,* he thought, *that was my motto, all right: "It's not what you say; it's how you say it." I guess I got you into this mess, Mitch. Now I need to get you out of it.*

"The green is clear. Let's hit first, then talk," he said.

Harry squared his shoulders as they walked toward the green together. "Back then, I thought I was doing you a favor, Mitch, but I was wrong. Yes, I believed that selling was fundamentally about the gift of gab. I got by on it for years, and so did you, because we're both unusually good at it. But I know now that it isn't *what you say*, and it isn't *how you say it*, either. It's what you *ask* that makes the

*"It isn't what you say and it isn't how you say it. It's what you ask."* difference between success and failure. Everything—the whole ball of wax—is about what you ask. Want to know how those other sales reps took away your business without discounting? I can tell

you in three words: *They asked questions!*"

Mitch couldn't believe his ears. "Give me a break! You mean I should qualify prospects? I said my career is in trouble, Harry, I didn't say I just fell off a turnip truck. *Of course* I ask questions—whenever they give me five minutes to do it!"

Harry shook his head. "No, you only think you ask questions. Fact is, you don't ask the right questions at the right times and in the right way to give you the information you need before your talking skills can even begin to help you."

"How would you know?" Mitch asked.

"I know from every single thing you've told me," Harry replied. "I don't really have to ask this, but have you heard of Action Selling?"

"What's that, one of those sales-training programs you always laugh at? I could use a laugh right now."

"It's a sales system, yeah. But this one I didn't laugh at, Mitch. This one saved *my* career."

"What are you talking about? You never had any…"

Harry cut him off. "This trouble you're talking about? This thing where suddenly the old charm isn't working anymore? It hit me about a year before it evidently hit you."

Mitch stared in disbelief.

"I'm dead serious," Harry said, marking his ball about 15 feet from the hole. "A few years ago I *was* you"—*a chatty dinosaur, gabbing my way toward extinction*, he thought—"my volume down, struggling to add new accounts, nobody with the time to talk to me. Or rather, to listen to me talk. I decided that maybe I was getting stale in the same old job—I had worked in the same place for six years. So I switched companies, partly for the change, partly

*"A few years ago I was you—a chatty dinosaur."*

because I figured I'd better move on while I still had what was left of my reputation as a top sales rep. I told you about the company I work for now."

Yes, part of their earlier conversation had been about Harry's new firm. He'd said he liked it there.

"Turned out they use a system called Action Selling," Harry said. "The first thing they did was to put me in a course. You can imagine how I felt about that."

Mitch smiled despite himself, remembering the sarcasm Harry used to heap on sales-training programs he was forced to attend. Harry claimed he could tell what a sales vice president had been eating for breakfast by the gimmicks expounded in the seminar the VP decided everyone needed *this* month.

Mitch's chip stopped two feet from the hole. "Nice shot," Harry said. Then he continued, "Well, I went in expecting the same old stuff. But I came out of this one realizing that I'd been selling for

*"I was just a seasoned amateur."*

more than 20 years, and I had never actually known squat about how to manage a sales call. I was just a seasoned amateur, and that wasn't cutting it anymore."

Harry sunk a long birdie putt on the fourth green, and then stood up straight with the putter dangling from his hand. "A few years ago I couldn't imagine saying something like this about a sales program with a straight face. But, Mitch, my friend, I stand before you today as a Certified Action Selling professional. That's why I know that you don't understand a thing about asking questions. And that you'll never dig yourself out of the hole you're in until you do."

"I guess you'd better tell me about it," Mitch said. "What have I got to lose?"

"Wrong question," Harry muttered under his breath. *You don't know it yet, Mitch, but this is about what you have to gain.*

# Chapter 1

## THE GABBY DINOSAUR

*Your terrific pitch—and where to pitch it.*

They teed off on the fifth hole, a long Par 5, and put away their drivers. "So," Mitch said, "as a Certified Action Selling professional, you can tell me how to ask—how'd you put it?—the right questions at the right times in the right way? That's what Action Selling is?"

"That's the heart of it," Harry said amiably. "Oh, Action Selling taught me a few other things I didn't know despite 20 years in the field. Like how to manage not just a sales call, but also the whole sales process. And how to match the selling process to the customer's buying process. And how to really plan and orchestrate sales calls so customers see me as a consultant and business partner, instead of just a guy who pitches the same commodities they can buy from anybody else.

"I've changed a lot about my selling game," Harry continued. "But if we're talking about how to *do* all of it, then, yes, Action

*"How to match the selling process to the customer's buying process."*

Selling keeps coming back to when and how to ask the best questions."

"OK, I'll bite," Mitch said. "When and how do I ask the best questions?"

Harry paused to examine a bad lie in the rough. He took a pitching wedge and knocked his ball back onto the fairway. "It would help if I had a clear picture of what you're doing now," he said. "For instance, you're not landing new accounts. You used to be very good at that. Any thoughts about what's changed?"

"Nothing much besides what I told you. The time-crunch thing is a big part of it. But even when a prospect gives me a decent amount of time, I just don't seem able to establish the level of credibility I used to get."

*"I just don't seem able to establish the level of credibility I used to get."*

"Tell you what," Harry said. "Walk me through an example of a recent call on a new account—one where you figured you had a good shot at getting the business."

Mitch didn't need long to think, as he laid up with a five iron. "All right, here's one. I was calling on Cheryl Gross, the technology buyer at Currentech. She's new in the role; they just hired her from outside. She called us in to bid on her business. Huge outfit. They buy about $2 million a year in product.

"Cheryl is one of these Type A personalities I see more and more, not interested in relationship stuff. You say that selling is all about questions now, Harry? Here's how Cheryl started our meeting.

She said, 'We've got 15 minutes, and I have three questions: What's the lead time? What's your price? And why should I buy from you?'"

"Harry, I gave her great answers! But it didn't matter. She still bought from a competitor. I heard they installed an elaborate system for ordering and tracking inventory—the whole nine yards."

"You say Cheryl is new," Harry said. "What did she do before she went to Currentech?"

"I don't know. She only gave me 15 minutes."

> *"I gave her great answers! She still bought from a competitor."*

Harry winced. "Other than delivery and price, what needs did she have?"

"She didn't explain any other needs. I thought that I would get more time with her in a future meeting. So I just did what she asked me to do."

A mocking voice in Harry's head repeated, *Of course I question them about their needs! I didn't just fall off a turnip truck!*

Sensing the direction of Harry's thoughts, Mitch reddened. "I tried to present our capabilities—the ones I felt would be most appealing. But they didn't seem to resonate. She actually looked at her watch twice during our meeting. I think she just brought me in to get a competitive bid that would justify a decision she already had made."

> *"Our capabilities... didn't seem to resonate."*

"That's possible," Harry said, as if he didn't find it especially relevant. "Tell me, if the meeting was 15 minutes long, how many minutes did you talk and how many minutes did she talk?"

"She never said much at all. After I answered her question about why she should buy from me, I asked if she thought the capabilities I'd described would be helpful. Know what she said? She said: 'Yes. How will you price your products for us?'"

"So, how many minutes did you talk out of 15?"

Mitch waved his arms in exasperation. "Maybe 14, all right?"

"How did you answer her price question, Mitch?"

"I offered her a 30 percent discount. That left me about 8 percent in gross margin. Which doesn't leave me with a whole lot of commission since I'm paid on gross margin."

Harry winced again. "Who, besides Cheryl, would be involved in making the decision on which supplier to select? Who has the budget? Who manages the people who will use the products? Who evaluates the technical aspects of your solution vs. the competition's?"

"I'm not sure if anyone else is involved," Mitch replied. "She didn't say."

*You mean you didn't ask*, Harry thought. "Which of your competitors did Cheryl look at?"

"She wouldn't tell me. I heard from a supplier that she bought from Genco."

"After you had this meeting, what communication did you have with her?" Harry asked.

"We exchanged some emails. And I emailed her a PowerPoint proposal. Did a nice job on it, too. But like I said, Harry, I think she had already decided, and the whole thing was a foregone conclusion. About two weeks later she sent me an email thanking me for the proposal and rejecting my offer."

Harry pulled a club out of his bag and began to swing it one-handed as they walked, back and forth, clipping the top of the grass like a scythe.

"Let me see if I understand this," he said finally. "A prospect who spends $2 million a year on equipment told you she had 15 minutes to discuss how to spend it. You accepted that at face value. Of those 15 minutes, you talked for 14. She asked three questions, you asked one. And your question was about how much she liked the talking you'd done. Am I right so far?"

> *"A prospect who spends $2 million a year told you she had 15 minutes to discuss how to spend it."*

*You asked for his help*, Mitch told himself. *But I didn't think it would be this painful.* "All right, yes," he said.

"Cheryl controlled everything about the call—the pace, what was discussed, the order in which things were discussed. Instead of asking you those three questions, she might just as easily have said, 'In 15 minutes or less, give me your standard pitch.' Because that's all she got from you."

"Well, gee, Harry, pardon me for answering a customer's questions. What are you going to tell me that Action Selling has some manipulative gimmicks that are supposed to let me dodge them instead? You used to sneer at that junk. I don't know who you've been calling on, but the customers I see today are *more* aware of manipulative sales tricks, not less."

*"Customers I see today are more aware of manipulative sales tricks."*

"You couldn't be further off base, Mitch," Harry said. "Trust me, I'm not pushing a method that assumes customers are idiots who won't see you coming a mile away with some little bag of gimmicks. Bear with me. Right now, I'm just trying to be sure I understand what happened on this sales call." *More to the point, I want you to understand what happened*, he thought.

Mitch plum-bobbed a long putt. "OK. Sorry, Harry."

*It's tough to be told you're not a professional*, Harry thought. *Believe me, I've been there*. "As I understand it," he said aloud,

*It's tough to be told you're not a professional.*

"here's what happened in terms of outcomes: Cheryl took control of your sales call the moment she uttered her first words about how little time she had."

"Yes," Mitch replied grimly.

"And all you learned about Cheryl or her company is that she is a Type A personality who assumes you're selling interchangeable commodities and that your pitch is all she needs to learn from you. You didn't find out where she worked or what she did before she took this job at Currentech. You didn't find out if anyone else would be involved in the buying decision and in what capacity. You didn't find out which suppliers you were competing against. You didn't learn anything about the particular problems or opportunities she needed to address with this purchase—not even why she felt lead-time was important. You didn't learn which factors in the buying decision would make this a real win to her company. You didn't learn how she, personally, might benefit from choosing the right solution or suffer from choosing the wrong one. Am I right about all of that?"

Mitch's defensiveness was rising again. "Yes, yes, yes, Harry, it's all true! But weren't you listening? She didn't give me a chance to ask her any questions!"

Harry seemed to consider the point. "Mitch, if you truly only had 15 minutes, did you think, in your wildest dreams, that you could land a $2 million deal with someone you didn't even know?"

> *"She didn't give me a chance to ask her any questions!"*

Mitch considered. "All right, but that doesn't change the basic situation. Cheryl said she had 15 minutes and told me exactly what she wanted to know. I was just responding to my customer. What non-manipulative, non-gimmicky thing should I have done instead of answering her questions?"

"Let's think about that," Harry replied. "She asked you three questions: lead-time, price, and why she should buy from you. Which of those questions was most important to you—and at least should have been most important to her?"

"'Why should I buy from you?' of course," Mitch said.

"And is that the one you spent the most time answering? I mean, if you talked for 14 minutes, I'll bet you spent 12 or 13 of them on why she should buy from you."

Mitch just nodded.

"Well, I would argue—and Action Selling would argue—that you were completely unqualified to answer that question. You knew

*"Why buy from you? You were completely unqualified to answer that question."*

nothing about Cheryl's situation, or her company's needs, or what Currentech hoped to gain from this purchase, or what's in it for Cheryl to make the right choice for Currentech. You couldn't connect any of the features and bene-fits of your products, services, or value-add offers to her real needs. Unless your company is extremely unusual, those generic features and benefits are a lot like the competition's.

"So, Mitch, how the heck would you know why Cheryl should buy from you? A Certified Action Selling professional would tell you that neither of you even knew *what* she was buying or what you were selling—which makes me wonder how you could answer her questions about price or lead-time, either."

Mitch looked at Harry thoughtfully. Then he silently walked off to take his next shot. When he caught up to Harry walking down the fairway, he said, "All right, that makes sense. For one thing, I see now that I let Cheryl take complete control of the call. I know bet-ter than that. But Harry, the issue remains: A customer tells me she has just a few minutes. She makes it plain what she wants to know and asks me a question—or three. I don't want to answer yet. What do I do to regain control without resorting to some bag of manipulative tricks?"

Harry smiled as if there were no mystery at all. "Why not tell her the simple truth?" he asked. "Suppose you said: 'Cheryl, at this point I'm not exactly sure why you should buy from me. But, I can tell you that, customers just like you buy from me for a lot of good reasons. So I can share the most relevant information, would you mind if I asked you a couple of questions?'"

Mitch looked around at the lush green golf course and the lovely blue sky. He tried to calculate the number of calls he had made in the past 18 months without landing a single account. He thought about how many had followed the same pattern as his call on Currentech. He thought about his desperate efforts to regain his past glory, all of them focused in one way or another on improving his talking skills. And he remembered the Harry he used to know. *Boy, are you singing a different tune.*

"Now let me guess," Mitch said. "If I spend the whole 15 minutes asking questions and never get to do any selling, she might discover she has more time if *she* gets to talk."

"That's certainly possible—either that, or she'd be more willing to make more time for you later. Except I'd also tell you that when you're asking questions, Mitch, you *are* selling. In fact, I'd tell you that almost all of the important 'selling' you do takes place while you're asking questions. I don't think there's any such thing as, 'I only asked questions and didn't get to do any selling.' On the other hand, I think these past few years you've been seeing the results you get from thinking, 'I have no time to ask questions because I'm too busy 'selling.'"

Mitch thought it over. "So, according to the new Harry, the Action Selling Certified Harry, it's not what you say, and it's not how you say it. It's what you ask?"

> *"When you're asking questions, you are selling."*

"Let's put it this way," Harry said. "Might your call on Cheryl have been more successful if it was aimed at solving *her* personal needs and not just at your idea of a typical customer?"

"That makes sense," Mitch said.

"Well, in that case, my answer to your question is yes: It isn't what you say or how you say it. It's what you ask."

> *"It isn't what you say or how you say it. It's what you ask."*

Mitch seemed lost in thought, taking his time with another putt. "I think maybe you'd better tell me more about Action Selling," he finally said.

"I think so too," Harry said. "But not here. I want to show you a kind of road map, a diagram that helps explain it. Plus, that four-some behind is getting impatient. What do you say we just try to finish this game without scoring in triple digits? Then you come to my office next week. Think you could find the time?" *Gabbing through sales calls is a hard habit to break, Mitch,* he thought. *But if I could do it, maybe you can too.*

"Oh, yeah," said Mitch, seeing a glimmer of hope at the end of a long, bleak tunnel. "Yeah, Harry, I can find the time."

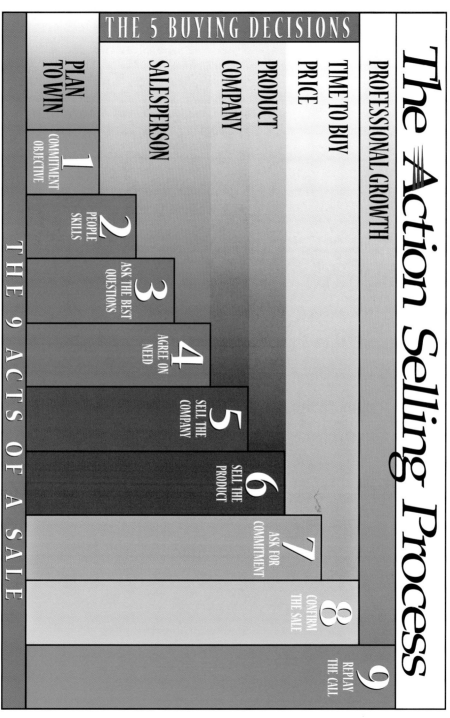

# The Action Selling Process

## THE 5 BUYING DECISIONS

PROFESSIONAL GROWTH

- SALESPERSON
- COMPANY
- PRODUCT
- PRICE
- TIME TO BUY

## THE 9 ACTS OF A SALE

**PLAN TO WIN**

1. COMMITMENT OBJECTIVE
2. PEOPLE SKILLS
3. ASK THE BEST QUESTIONS
4. AGREE ON NEED
5. SELL THE COMPANY
6. SELL THE PRODUCT
7. ASK FOR COMMITMENT
8. CONFIRM THE SALE
9. REPLAY THE CALL

# Action Selling

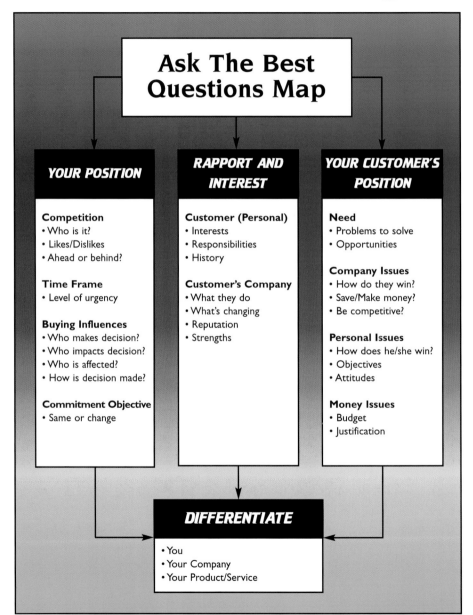

## Ask The Best Questions Map

### YOUR POSITION

**Competition**
• Who is it?
• Likes/Dislikes
• Ahead or behind?

**Time Frame**
• Level of urgency

**Buying Influences**
• Who makes decision?
• Who impacts decision?
• Who is affected?
• How is decision made?

**Commitment Objective**
• Same or change

### RAPPORT AND INTEREST

**Customer (Personal)**
• Interests
• Responsibilities
• History

**Customer's Company**
• What they do
• What's changing
• Reputation
• Strengths

### YOUR CUSTOMER'S POSITION

**Need**
• Problems to solve
• Opportunities

**Company Issues**
• How do they win?
• Save/Make money?
• Be competitive?

**Personal Issues**
• How does he/she win?
• Objectives
• Attitudes

**Money Issues**
• Budget
• Justification

### DIFFERENTIATE

• You
• Your Company
• Your Product/Service

# Chapter 2

## THE PROFESSIONAL'S BLUEPRINT

### *How Harry saved his career*

Mitch walked into Harry's office and was stunned by the view through the floor-to-ceiling windows of the first hole at Bear Creek Country Club.

He whistled in appreciation. "They treat you pretty well here, Harry. You didn't tell me you get to study golf every day. No wonder you beat me like a drum."

They stood at the windows and watched a player tee off on number one and slice a drive far into the ninth fairway. "That guy hits it like me," Mitch said.

"You had something else on your mind when we played," Harry replied, grinning. "If we can put your selling game on track, maybe your golf game will improve too. Then I won't feel so bad taking your money the next time we tee it up. Want to get to it?"

They moved to a small conference table across the room from

Harry's desk. "I've been thinking about our conversation last week, and something puzzles me," Mitch said. "The things you said about my call on Cheryl Gross made a lot of sense. But how were you able to diagnose the problems so quickly? I've been trying for two years to figure out what's wrong, and no luck. When I described that sales

*"How were you able to diagnose my selling problems so quickly?"*

call to you it was as if you had a checklist of mistakes in your head and you could just watch me make them, one after the other. It was weird that you could give me the kind of analysis you did so quickly. How did you do it?"

"Simple," Harry said. "Two words: Action Selling. Like I told you, Mitch, it's taken my selling game to an entirely new level. Like you, I knew a lot about selling. But today, I've got a systematic approach to managing a sales call—and the whole sales process, from planning to following up. Once you understand it, you'll have a framework that lets you diagnose and correct your own selling errors—like a navigation system that tells you when you've lost your way."

"Yes, you said there was more to it than asking questions."

*"I've got a systematic approach—a navigation system that tells you when you've lost your way."*

"Think of it this way," Harry said. "Action Selling is a research-based system that tells you, step by step, how to win over new cus-

tomers and keep the ones you've already got. On one level, asking questions is just part of the process. But on another level, it's the whole ballgame—because success at every step hinges on the quality of the questions you ask.

"You're fighting a battle out there, Mitch, and the battlefield is the customer's mind. Your ultimate goal is to win customers who are loyal enough to *stop shopping* for a better deal because they're persuaded that you have become their business partner. And when I say 'you,' I mean you—not your company, not your products, not your presentation, and not your price. You used to be able to differentiate yourself from the competition based on your product features and your skill at describing them. But practically all products and services are perceived as commodities nowadays; there's not much real difference between yours and the next guy's.

"I used to claim that it's not what you say, it's how you say it. Today I'd tell you that the game isn't about what you *say*, it's about what you *ask*. Selling isn't telling. The only way to gain a lasting competitive advantage today is to get customers to perceive you

> *"You're fighting a battle, and the battlefield is the customer's mind."*

as a valuable consultant and partner instead of just another salesperson with a product pitch.

"Action Selling gives you a proven plan for becoming that kind of consultant," Harry continued. "The keys that let you execute the plan are questioning and listening—not talking. You said that any salesperson who didn't just fall off a turnip truck knows he's supposed to ask questions to qualify a customer. But most salespeople are amateurs at questioning, no matter how long they've been selling. The professional, who wins against the competition, is the one who understands that selling is a process, who always knows what point he's at in that process, who asks the *best* questions at every

*"The keys that let you execute the plan are questioning and listening."*

step, and who knows what to do next with the answers he hears. Execute that process better than your competitors do, and you win. Period."

Mitch studied Harry. "You're really sold on Action Selling, aren't you?"

"Like I told you, it saved my career," Harry said.

"So explain it to me. I'm ready."

*"Action Selling saved my career."*

Harry opened his day planner and took out a colorful laminated card and a blank page. He drew something quickly on the page. When he turned it around, Mitch saw a question mark divided into sections.

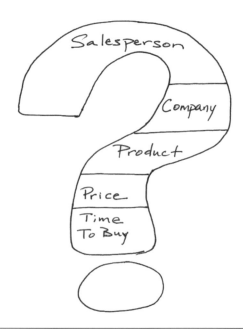

"Action Selling is based on a documented fact," Harry began. "In the course of any major sale, every customer makes five crucial buying decisions. These decisions are always made in a predetermined order."

First, Harry explained, the customer decides whether to "buy" the salesperson. "Does she like me? Does she trust me? Am I the person she wants to buy from?

"What do you notice about the salesperson portion of the question mark?" Harry asked.

"It's larger than the rest."

"That's right. Whether to buy the salesperson is not just the first decision a customer makes, it's the most important one. Everything else depends on it. That's what determines whether somebody like Cheryl Gross will decide that maybe you're worth more than 15 minutes of her time after all."

> *"Whether to buy the salesperson is not just the first decision, it's the most important one."*

After customers have "bought" the salesperson, Harry explained, they make a decision about the company he represents: Is it reputable? Is it a good match for the customer's company?

Then they consider the product: Is it the right solution for the customer's problem? How does it compare with competitive products?

Then they decide about the price: Is the product worth the money?

Finally, they consider the "time to buy": When do they want to take possession of the product? When does the buying decision actually need to be made?

"To summarize: In every major sale, customers make those five decisions in the same order," Harry said. "And customers will not seriously consider a later decision until the earlier ones have been made. For you, that means you can't sell your company or your product before you have sold yourself. For the customer, it means that trying to make those decisions in the wrong order leads to bad buying choices. Action Selling tells you how to manage a sales call so that the five decisions are considered in the proper order."

"But what about customers like Cheryl?" Mitch asked. "She sure didn't seem to be thinking of those decisions in that order."

"It's common that buyers like Cheryl will start out sounding as if price and delivery are the primary decisions. But remember when she asked, 'Why should I buy from you?' What decision was she considering?"

*"Action Selling says that every sales call is like a drama with nine acts."*

"Probably the salesperson and company," said Mitch. "So, what does Action Selling tell me to do?"

"Action Selling says that every sales call is like a drama with nine acts," Harry said. "The salesperson has to be the director who keeps things moving in the right order. The order follows the sequence of the 5 Buying Decisions." Tapping the laminated card in front of Mitch, he explained the Action Selling system like this:

**Act 1: Commitment Objective**. This act is like a prelude to the drama. Before any sales call begins, the salesperson first must determine a Commitment Objective for the call. A Commitment Objective is a goal that specifies an action the customer should agree to take— something you want the customer to agree to do that will move the sales process forward.

> *A Commitment Objective specifies an action the customer should agree to take.*

"'I'll go in and deliver my pitch' is not a Commitment Objective because it requires no action from the customer," Harry said. He explained that at some point in the process, the Commitment Objective will be to get the customer to agree to buy the product. But in the early stages, the Commitment Objective more often will be something like getting the customer to agree to schedule another meeting with other decision-makers who will play a role in the buying process.

Action Selling insists that it is unprofessional to call on a customer without a specific Commitment Objective in mind, Harry told Mitch, because if a call doesn't move the process forward in some way then it wastes the customer's time as well as the salesperson's. "No Commitment Objective, no call," Harry said.

> *"Thinking you could get a $2 million deal during your first meeting was a stretch."*

"Since every call needs a Commitment Objective, you need to determine what you can realistically achieve. Maybe the idea that you could get a $2 million deal during your first meeting with Cheryl Gross was a stretch."

"Yeah, in 15 minutes. What was I thinking?" Mitch mumbled.

"Questions come into play here because you have to ask yourself good questions about what a reasonable Commitment Objective would be," Harry continued. "Then, the questions you ask the customer during the call may give you cues that your Commitment Objective needs to change. But if that happens, you always pick a new Commitment Objective. You never abandon the goal of getting the customer to agree to take some action. You never forget that that's ultimately why you're there."

"So, agreeing on a longer meeting would have been a good Commitment Objective with Cheryl?" Mitch asked, taking notes.

"It would have been more realistic," Harry agreed.

**Act 2: People Skills**. This act opens the actual call. The salesperson begins to address the customer's first major buying decision—that is, the salesperson starts to "sell himself" by demonstrating that he is likeable, credible, and trustworthy.

"You've been trying to do that mostly by talking, just as I used to," Harry told Mitch. "But the actual key to it is *listening*. You ask open-ended questions that encourage the *customer* to do the talking—about herself, her background, and her company.

"Considering Cheryl's get-down-to-business style, a lot of Act 2 conversation is probably not going to happen," Harry conceded. "But asking about her new position or perhaps where she had worked prior to Currentech might have been a good idea."

"I can see that, Harry," said Mitch. "But she caught me off guard when she started the meeting the way she did."

"That's all the more reason why you need to have a questioning plan going into a sales call. With a questions plan you're better able to respond to the curve balls that get thrown at you."

*"With a questions plan you're better able to respond to curve balls."*

Act 2 is the first of three acts that Action Selling devotes to the customer's first major buying decision, Harry explained. "That's how crucial it is to 'sell yourself.'"

**Act 3: Ask the Best Questions**. Having established rapport and shown interest in learning something about the customer, the salesperson begins to zero in on gaining a better understanding of the customer's situation. Action Selling teaches that most of the "selling" that occurs in any call actually takes place in Act 3—before salespeople present their product.

"In other words, the majority of the selling is happening when the customer is doing most of the talking," Harry said.

"I've never thought of it that way," Mitch said. "I've always felt that I had to be persuasive—like I had to change their thinking. You make it sound like buyers are more open-minded than I think they are."

*"Most of the selling is happening when the customer is doing the talking."*

"Yes. That's exactly how Action Selling works. A sale needs to be 'opened' before it can be 'closed.' When it's done properly, the questioning process opens the customer's mind. While you are thoroughly and creatively exploring the customer's situation, they become open to doing business with you."

"I can see that in an ideal situation, Harry. But Cheryl wasn't in that frame of mind. 'What?' 'How much?' and 'Why you?' doesn't exactly suggest an open mind."

Harry considered Mitch's comment. *You don't sound open to what I'm telling you, either*, he thought. *I should practice what I preach and ask some questions.* Out loud, he said, "Let me ask, Mitch, how would you categorize the success of your meeting with Cheryl using the approach that you took?"

Mitch was stopped in his tracks. He realized that Harry wasn't going to buy his argument that his selling situation was unique. "It was a complete failure," he admitted.

"What I'm sharing with you won't work every time. But from my recent experience, when Action Selling is done properly, the results are amazing. I heard an interview with Tiger Woods where they asked him how he could hit the ball so well in the wind at the British Open. He said something like, 'When you hit the ball properly, the wind doesn't have that much effect.' What I'm telling you, Mitch, is that when you follow this sales process, the tough situations you're describing are manageable."

> *"With this sales process, the tough situations are manageable."*

Mitch, feeling a little embarrassed, turned over the laminated card to look at the "Ask the Best Questions Map" on the other side.

"Hold on," Harry said. "A lot of what Action Selling has to teach you about questions pertains to that map and to Act 3. For now, let's just say that Asking the Best Questions at this point in the sales process gives you the information you need to complete the next six acts of the drama. Act 3 is where you find out how the customer's buying process works and who else might be involved. It's also where you learn about the real key needs that your solution will have to address.

"In other words," Harry continued, "Act 3 is where you find out how you're going to present your company and your products to *this* customer so that you sound like a consultant with a solution instead of a generic salesperson with a generic pitch for a commodity product that the customer probably could buy cheaper from someone else."

*"I open the customer's mind to doing business by asking the best questions."*

"Wait a second," Mitch said, catching up with his note taking. "So I open the customer's mind to doing business with me by asking the best questions? Okay, go ahead."

**Act 4: Agree on Need**. One primary goal of Asking the Best Questions is to uncover at least three unique, important needs that the salesperson's products could address. In Act 4, which is short but crucial, the salesperson confirms his understanding of those needs. He does this, Harry explained, simply by saying: "As I understand it, you're looking for a solution that will do X, Y, and Z. Is that correct?"

This helps the salesperson "sell himself" by demonstrating that he has listened carefully to the customer's explanation of her needs. It also cements and clarifies those needs in the customer's own mind.

"Above all," Harry said, "it allows the salesperson to focus everything else he says and does upon specific needs that the customer has already agreed are important. Until you have agreed on needs with a customer, Mitch, *you don't know how* to present your company or your products as anything but commodities."

"This is different from how I've always done it—and how we used to do it when you first showed me the ropes," Mitch said. "We would find a need and fill it. Then we'd find another one and fill it."

> *"Until you have agreed on needs, you don't know how to present anything but commodities."*

"That's right," Harry confirmed. "With Act 4, we don't get ahead of ourselves. We thoroughly analyze the customer's situation before we present. This avoids selling errors that cause resistance later in the call."

Harry smiled at Mitch. "You'll like the next parts," he said. "Here comes your chance to gab a little. But the thing is, now you don't have to gab nearly as much."

**Act 5: Sell the Company**. Until this point in the call, the customer has done the vast majority of the talking. And by encouraging that to happen while listening carefully, the salesperson has been "selling himself." Now it's time to address the customer's second major buying decision—the one about whether to "buy" the salesperson's company.

"To sell your company, you describe its reputation and its capabilities," Harry said. "But you can throw out most of your canned presentation, and do this more briefly and powerfully. Why? Because now you can focus your description on some of the specific needs that you and the customer have agreed upon. You're now able to tell this individual what your company can do to solve *her* problems—especially, why your company is a perfect match for hers."

**Act 6: Sell the Product**. In the same manner, the salesperson presents his products or services not with a canned presentation, but in a way that specifically illustrates how they would address the key needs agreed upon in Act 4.

"This is much quicker than a data-dump pitch where you present a lot of product features the customer doesn't care about, hoping that something will interest her because it once interested somebody else," Harry said. "It's also far more effective. You'll do less talking than you're used to, but what you say will mean a whole lot more to the customer."

> *"You'll do less talking, but what you say will mean a whole lot more."*

Mitch looked up from his notes and grinned. "To sell myself, I let the customer talk. To sell my company and my products, I talk, but I don't blabber. Is that it?"

"You got it."

"But this sounds harder to do because I can't practice my pitch ahead of the call. I'll need to custom-tailor each product presentation as I deliver it."

"Yes, you will," Harry agreed. "But at the same time, you'll deliver a much more powerful message because it zeros in on the customer's unique situation."

**Act 7: Ask for Commitment**. Before the call began, the salesperson established a Commitment Objective. He may have changed it as new information was revealed, but he still wants the customer to agree to take some action that will move the sales process forward.

"If the commitment you want from the customer is to purchase your product," Harry said, "first you quickly summarize the product features that corresponded to the customer's key needs. Then you quote the price. Then, immediately, you ask, 'How does that sound?' If the customer agrees that it sounds good, you ask, 'Would you like to go ahead with it?'

"If your Commitment Objective is to schedule another meeting, then, instead of a price, you quote the time needed for that meeting. The 'features' you summarize are about what the customer will gain by meeting with you."

"I understand," Mitch said, making a note.

**Act 8: Confirm the Sale**. If the customer agrees, the salesperson takes out a sort of insurance policy against buyer's remorse. This is a quick, three-step process, summed up by the terms *assure, appreciate*, and *future event*. First, *assure* the customer that she has made the right decision. Then thank her and tell her you *appreciate* her commitment. Then schedule a *future event* that the customer can look forward to instead of worrying about the commitment she made.

"The future event is a neat concept," Harry said. "You'll learn about that when you start to pursue Action Selling Certification yourself—which you're going to want to do."

Mitch had been thinking the same thing for several minutes.

**Act 9: Replay the Call**. After every sales call, without exception, the salesperson conducts a mental review to identify what he did well during each act and what he should have done better.

"Remember when you said I analyzed your call on Cheryl Gross as if I had a mental checklist of mistakes I could watch you make?" Harry asked. "You should have a pretty good idea by now where that checklist came from. But I have a lot of practice in using it because I apply it to myself after every sales call I make. I didn't learn the Action Selling system once, improve my skills, and then plateau again. By replaying my calls, I keep getting more and more effective. The improvement never ends."

Mitch made a final note and leaned back in his chair. "I appreciate this, Harry," he said. "Even if I walked out of here right now, I think I'd be a lot better off than I was. But if I understand you right,

> *"The thing that lets me climb the steps is questioning skills."*

these nine acts are the basic steps in the process. The thing that really lets me climb the steps is questioning skills. Is that right?"

"Right."

"And you and Action Selling have more to tell me about questioning skills?" He pointed again to the Ask the Best Questions Map on the other side of the laminated card.

"Right again."

"Then tell me, please."

So Harry did.

# Chapter 3

## THE "NEW" ART OF SELLING

*Mapping out a masterpiece.*

Harry picked up the laminated card. He looked at one side, then the other, as if searching for something he hadn't seen before. Then he spoke.

"Mitch, I'm wondering how to explain the significance of what I'm holding in my hand. If we just dig straight into the details, you could miss the enormity of these ideas and what they mean to the future of our profession."

Mitch examined his long-time mentor, wondering if he had slipped off the deep end. But no, Harry seemed serious and sober.

"What I've got in my hand is like a thousand great ideas all rolled into one system," Harry said. "But you can't really see that until you completely understand the Action Selling process. A lot of my coworkers have taken an idea or two from Action Selling and improved their game. But some of us have grasped the whole picture. When that happens, it's like being enlightened.

"The enlightened learn from Action Selling every day. It's as if the process gives us this magical framework or operating system from which we solve selling problems and grow our skills. Parts of

*The enlightened learn from Action Selling every day."*

the system, like the way it's structured around the five buying decisions, are based on research or 'science.' But we think of the questioning portion of Action Selling as the 'artful' part of selling today. We create or design questions and use them to make masterful sales calls. The benefits we've experienced are enormous."

Harry pulled another page out of his planner and began to jot some notes.

## QUESTIONS BENEFITS

- Open the Sale = Close the Sale
- Sells the Salesperson
  - Consultant
  - Interested
  - Thorough
  - Thoughtful
- Learn "What" and "How" to Sell
- Differentiate You, Company, Product
- Build Emotion & Logic
- Qualify - Improve Time Management
- Balance Communications Process
- Earn the Right to Ask

Harry then started to talk Mitch through the notes he had made.

"Most salespeople think their biggest problem is closing sales," he said. "In fact, the reason they can't close is because they never *opened* the sale properly. Asking questions is how you do that."

> *"The reason they can't* **close** *is because they* **never opened."**

He tapped the next point on his list. "Questioning the client is how you 'sell yourself.' It shows that you're interested in the customer's problems, you want to understand them thoroughly, and you're *thinking* about how you can help. In a word, you're acting like a real consultant."

Tap. "No matter what your product is, until you ask the right questions you don't know either *what* you're selling or *how* to sell it. If you think you do, you're peddling a commodity, pure and simple."

Tap. "Asking questions is the only way to differentiate yourself, your products, and your company. You can't talk your way out of the commodity trap. You can only ask your way out."

Tap. "Questions tell you where the customer's hot buttons are, on both logical and emotional levels. Those are the buttons your presentation has to push."

Tap. "Questions are how you qualify customers and quit wasting your time trying to sell to the wrong people."

Tap. "Questions balance the communication process by allowing you to have a two-way conversation with the customer instead of a situation where they just listen to as much of your monologue as they're willing to stand."

Tap. "Finally, what gives you the right to ask all these questions? After all, you're just a salesperson. The answer is that you don't *have* the right, you *earn* the right. Every time you ask a good question—one that shows you to be a thoughtful consultant who wants to understand and help improve the client's business—you earn the right to ask another question. And then another. And then another."

> **"You earn the right every time you ask a good question."**

Harry laid down his pen and picked up the laminated card again. "Mitch, the salesperson who does all of that best, wins. This is called the 'Best Questions Map' because it lets you be the best—by helping you ask the best questions."

He paused to let that sink in. "Now, the Best Questions are open-ended. You know what those are?"

"They can't be answered with a yes or no. Yeah I know that," Mitch responded.

"Research shows that open-ended questions are critical to success *in and of themselves*—I mean, even disregarding the quality or cleverness or value of the actual questions. Calls with more open-ended questions than close-ended ones are 25 percent more successful. What do you make of that?"

> **"Calls with more open-ended questions are 25 percent more successful."**

"I didn't know that. But I know we need to use them to get the customer talking— so we can be better at listening," Mitch said.

*So you understand the concept of open-ended questions, you just don't put it into practice during sales calls, when it actually matters,* Harry thought. *Instead, you talk for 14 minutes out of 15.* Rather than jump Mitch about it now, he decided to wait.

Harry placed the laminated card on the table, leaned forward and tapped his finger on The Best Questions Map. "What do you make of this, Mitch?" he asked. "What does it seem to be telling you?"

Mitch studied the map. "It's an outline of different things I want to know about the customer and his company—or her company," he said, still thinking of Cheryl Gross. "And let me guess: The arrows pointing to the 'Differentiate' box at the bottom mean that the point of gathering the information in the top columns is to let me differentiate myself as a consultant rather than just another salesperson. It also lets me differentiate my company and products in, let's see…" (he consulted his notes) "…Acts 5 and 6, because I can present them as solutions to the specific needs the customer and I agreed upon in Act 4."

| **DIFFERENTIATE** |
|---|
| • You |
| • Your Company |
| • Your Product/Service |

Harry was pleased. "Nothing wrong with your listening skills, Mitch," he said.

"Except that I'm beginning to see I haven't used them nearly enough because I've been too busy gabbing," Mitch replied. He pointedly closed his mouth and looked at Harry expectantly, inviting him to go on speaking.

Harry smiled at Mitch's expression. "Okay, look at the middle column on the map, the one labeled *'Rapport and Interest.'* Think of those categories as things you'll ask about in Act 2, as a sales call begins, in order to build rapport with the customer. Suppose you could start over with Cheryl Gross. Well, who is she as a person? What can you learn about her? You already know Currentech hired her from somewhere else, so where did she work before? What did she do there? And what, exactly, does she do in her present job at Currentech?

---

**RAPPORT AND INTEREST**

**Customer (Personal)**
• Interests
• Responsibilities
• History

**Customer's Company**
• What they do
• What's changing
• Reputation
• Strengths

---

"Everybody's favorite subject is themselves," Harry said. "Most people will tell you about themselves if you just ask questions that encourage them to talk—and show that you're interested in what they say."

> *"People will tell you about themselves if you ask questions and show that you're interested."*

"Or pretend you're interested," Mitch said, grinning.

Harry just gave him a look and continued. "The more Cheryl talks about herself, the better you get to know her as an individual and not just as a 'Type A personality.' But you're there for a business purpose, so naturally you want to know about her company, as well. You'll have done some homework before the call, so you'll know something about Currentech and what it does—right?"

"Sure," Mitch assured him. "I mean, yes, I did some research on Currentech before I called on Cheryl."

"Okay," Harry said, "but you still want to get the picture from Cheryl's perspective. What challenges does Currentech face in its market? What's changing in its market? What are its competitive strengths and weaknesses? The answers to questions like those will give you information that you can use to describe the benefits of your product in terms that are most meaningful to your customer. Of course, you'll do this much later in the call."

Mitch recoiled, struck by a thought. "When I hear something that's connected to a benefit of my product, I go straight into my pitch."

> *"Ask, listen, be patient, and follow the process."*

"That's a classic selling error," Harry said. "Even if Cheryl essentially tells you to give her your pitch and leave, you're being presumptuous—as if you understand her business without asking anything about it. What's worse, if she gives you 15 minutes and you talk for 14, all you can do is describe a commodity that she can buy from someone else."

Angry at himself, Mitch jotted a note: *Ask, listen, be patient, and follow the process.*

Then he looked up and said, "Okay, Harry. What are the other columns on the Questions Map for?"

"Those columns move you from Act 2 to Act 3," Harry explained. "It isn't as if everything stops and then a curtain rises on Act 3; there's no big, dramatic pause. But now you turn the conversation naturally toward the specific issues driving the buying decision you're there to discuss. You need all the information you can get about two basic things: what you're going to sell, and how you're going to sell it. That's what the other two columns on the Questions Map are about."

"Harry, this could take a while," Mitch protested. "If she gives me 15 minutes, I couldn't possibly get all of this done, much less answer her questions."

Now Harry recoiled. *He either doesn't get it or he isn't buying into Action Selling.* "Look, Mitch," he said, "you've got to stop thinking that selling is telling. It's not. Selling is asking. Remember that the customer first must be sold on you. If you're talking up a storm about your product, the customer is forced to evaluate you based on information about your product. You're completely out of sync with the customer's buying decisions. You're doomed, and you'll lose if you don't change how you're thinking about this."

*"You've got to stop thinking that selling is telling. It's not."*

"Hey, Harry, old habits die hard," Mitch said, trying to lighten the conversation. "I slipped back in time again. I've got more than a few changes to make, and I'm having trouble keeping all of this in front of me. I'm here to learn what I need to do to get my game back on track."

Rather than add to his point, Harry reached forward again and tapped the column labeled "Your Position." He explained that the questions in that column help the salesperson understand how the customer's buying process works, what other parties will be involved in the buying decision, which competing vendors the customer is considering, and so on.

| YOUR POSITION |
| --- |
| **Competition** |
| • Who is it? |
| • Likes/Dislikes |
| • Ahead or behind? |
| |
| **Time Frame** |
| • Level of urgency |
| |
| **Buying Influences** |
| • Who makes decision? |
| • Who impacts decision? |
| • Who is affected? |
| • How is decision made? |
| |
| **Commitment Objective** |
| • Same or change |

"In other words," Harry said, "the questions in the 'Your Position' column uncover information about *how to sell* to this particular customer. How is this sales process going to evolve?"

For instance, Harry explained, the salesperson wants to know: Who is the customer's current supplier? What does she like and dislike about the service she's getting from that supplier? And what is the time frame for getting the product? That helps determine if the decision needs to be made tomorrow or six months from now.

"You also need to know if other players will be involved in the buying decision," Harry said. "Who besides Cheryl must be sold? Who has the budget authority to buy? And who else will be consulted about the decision: The employees who actually use the product? Their managers? Some technical specialists?

"Those are all questions that let you know *how to sell*," Harry continued. "The answers tell you if your Commitment Objective has to change. If your Commitment Objective for the call on Cheryl was to get her to agree to buy, and you find out that she can't or won't do that without consulting someone else, what do you suppose has to happen to your Commitment Objective?"

"I know exactly what you mean," Mitch said. "If I find out she's not the final decision-maker, my Commitment Objective becomes: Get her to agree to pass me on to the decision maker so I can make my presentation to him or her. Right?"

"Wrong," Harry said, causing Mitch to do a double-take. "That's another common selling error. A lot of salespeople think, 'If I could just go straight to the big boss, I could quit wasting my time talking to underlings.' Wrong, wrong, wrong. In the first place, you're not ready

> *"If I go straight to the boss, I quit wasting my time with underlings. Wrong."*

to make a presentation to *anybody* yet. In the second place, the big boss will rarely make a major buying decision without consulting anyone else. If Cheryl isn't the final decision-maker, that doesn't mean she's just some time-wasting obstacle you have to get around. More likely she could be a key ally to you in making the sale. So could the users and the technical specialists."

Mitch thought it over. "All right," he said, "if my new Commitment Objective isn't to get a meeting with the final decision-maker, what is it?"

"Well, how about this: Suppose you could get Cheryl to agree to put you in touch with *all* of the parties who will have a say in the buying decision, either together or separately. Not so that you can make a presentation to them, but so you can ask them the same kinds of questions you're going to ask Cheryl in this next column." Harry tapped the column labeled "Your Customer's Position."

---

**YOUR CUSTOMER'S POSITION**

**Need**
• Problems to solve
• Opportunities

**Company Issues**
• How do they win?
• Save/Make money?
• Be competitive?

**Personal Issues**
• How does he/she win?
• Objectives
• Attitudes

**Money Issues**
• Budget
• Justification

---

"The 'Customer's Position' column is the one with questions that are going to tell me *what* to sell?" Mitch asked.

"Yep. These are the kinds of issues you'll probe to uncover the key needs behind the five buying decisions. This is how you'll discover those needs you're going to agree upon with Cheryl in Act 4. And since you want to understand and agree on the needs of everyone with an important voice in the buying decision, you'll need access to all of them before you're ready to make a professional presentation."

"Hmmm," Mitch mused. "You said earlier that if I use Action Selling, I'll run into fewer objections when I finally ask customers to agree to buy. Let me guess some more: That's because I'm going to uncover a lot of potential objections with this questioning, aren't I? So when I make my presentation, I can anticipate and address them up front."

## *"I'm going to uncover a lot of potential objections with questioning."*

"Very good," Harry said. *You're a smart guy, Mitch*, he thought. *I didn't pick up on that as fast when I was learning the Action Selling system.* "When you present your company and your products, you'll be talking about how you will address specific needs that all parties to the buying decision have already agreed are the most important ones. You're a lot less likely to get sandbagged late in the game with an objection based on some issue you never heard about. You'll know *what to sell* because you're on the same page with the buyers about what's important and what isn't—so you can sell a solution to their needs instead of selling a generic commodity. Hence the term: *differentiate*."

"I get it," Mitch said, looking at the map. "Questions about issues in the 'Customer's Position' column let me find out things like why Cheryl cared so much about lead time."

"And how might knowing that affect your answer to *her* question about the kind of lead time you can offer—when you're ready to answer it, I mean?" Harry asked.

Mitch thought. "I think I see where you're going," he said. "For an account her size, we could accommodate any cycle she needs. I was an idiot to say, 'Our usual lead time is five days' and let it go at that."

"Look at the bright side," Harry said. "If that makes you an idiot, you've got a lot of company among the salespeople you compete with. But now you're going to know better."

Harry tapped the "Customer's Position" column again. "If you want to differentiate yourself as a consultant who is there to help, and not just to sell a gadget, you have to uncover the issues that actually drive the buying decision. What does Cheryl's company really stand to gain from this purchase? How can it save money? How can it make money? In other words, how does her company win if it makes the right decision?

"Beyond that," Harry continued, "how does Cheryl herself win if she makes a good choice? What problems are causing her pain? What opportunities could she grasp? What kind

> *"You have to uncover the issues that actually drive the buying decision."*

of solution would reduce her personal headaches and maybe even let her come out of the deal looking like a corporate hero? That's the solution you ultimately want to present. That's what you, your product, and your company should represent to her. That's *what to sell*.

And how do you discover the needs that would let you present that kind of solution?"

## *"Then I shut my big yap and listen."*

"I ask questions," Mitch replied, the light bulb in his head shining brightly now. "Then I shut my big yap and listen to the answers."

"Bingo," Harry said. "Now then, you know the purpose behind these questions. You know what kind of information you're trying to uncover. And you know what you're going to do with that information—namely, agree on needs with the customer and then craft a presentation about your company and your products that specifically address those needs. What questions do you have for me at this point?"

"I've got plenty," Mitch said, smiling like a good student. "How? I mean, you've told me the 'what.' Now, what does Action Selling have to say about *how* I should ask these questions so that I find out what I need to know?"

"Good question," Harry said. He looked at his watch. "What do you say we go have some lunch, then come back here and continue?"

# Chapter 4

## EARN THE RIGHT TO ASK

*Yeah, but how do you do it?*

"I still say you owe me five bucks," Harry deadpanned as they walked back into his office and saw the golf course spread below.

Mitch strangled a laugh, producing a small snort. He recovered himself and matched Harry's serious tone. "For the last time, it wasn't a real bet, Harry, it was an expression. 'Five bucks says the guy corkscrews himself right into the ground' is an *expression*."

While eating lunch on the terrace of the Bear Creek Country Club, they had watched a player with a truly unfortunate swing pull his drive off the first tee deep into the parking lot of Harry's office building, then take a mulligan and do the same thing again.

"That swing looked like it actually hurt," Harry said. " I hope you parked your car on the far end of the lot. I always do."

"Oh, I get it. My car is being pelted with golf balls and you want me to cough up five bucks," Mitch replied.

"Well, I can see you're never going to pay up, despite the way I'm saving your sorry career. Shall we get back to Action Selling?"

"Please," Mitch said, as they settled into their chairs. "I do appreciate this you know, Harry."

Harry smiled and waved away the gratitude. *It's more fun to bust your chops*, he thought.

"All right," Mitch said, "you told me the 'why' of asking all these questions, and the Best Questions Map tells me 'what' I need to find out. Now we're up to 'how.' If I'm following you, Action Selling can tell me how to ask 'The Best' open-ended questions in a way that uncovers 'The Best' customer needs." Mitch used his fingers to put quote marks around 'The Best' each time he said the

*"'The Best' open-ended questions uncover 'The Best' customer needs."* words. "After I have agreed on those needs with the customer, I can customize a presentation that lets me differentiate by selling directly to 'The Best' needs instead of delivering my standard pitch. Correct?"

"Yep," Harry said.

"Okay, on Thursday I have a call scheduled at Bridgeco. It's potentially a big account. The client's name is Jim Bradley. I've never met him, just talked to him on the phone to get the appointment. So here's an open-ended question: How do I go about questioning Bradley?"

"Good idea, let's use him as an example," Harry said. "You want to uncover needs that your products are well qualified to solve, right? If you're going to prepare some questions that would get Jim Bradley to think about needs like those, where do you suppose you'd start?"

Mitch thought for a moment. "With my products, I guess. My product features?"

"Very good. The needs you're looking for are ones that correspond to the strengths of your products, your services, or your company. So you'd start by identifying unique or differentiating features. What do you or your products do better than your competition does?"

Another pause from Mitch. "That ought to be an easy question," he finally said. "But actually, our products aren't that different from others on the market. We try to differentiate more around service and ancillary stuff."

"That's the usual situation these days," Harry said. "Almost all products have become commodities. And truth be told, I'll bet your service and your guarantees and your value-add offers aren't exactly unique either."

Mitch wiggled his hand in a "not exactly" gesture.

"Uh-huh," Harry said. "Which just proves the point that it isn't what you sell but how you sell that counts. All right, forget 'unique.' But what are you especially good at? What are your three cially good at? What are your three strongest capabilities—the ones that usually appeal most to your customers?"

> *"It isn't* **what** *you sell but* **how** *you sell that counts."*

With some prodding from Harry, Mitch settled on these three capabilities as the biggest differentiating factors he had to work with:

## STRENGTHS

- Best system for acquisition
- Easiest access to technical support
- Best customer education/certification

"Let me see if I understand," Harry said when they were through. "First, thanks to your integrated online system, customers can access your entire supply chain to order parts, components and programs. That's what 'best acquisition system' means. Second, your tech-support people are available 24/7 online, and your field technicians can be reached during working hours via cell phones. Third, your customer-education and certification programs are among the most respected in the industry, with the best courses and instructors. Those are the things you'd describe as your strongest differentiators?"

Mitch agreed with Harry's summary.

"So in the best of all possible worlds," Harry asked, "you would learn that Jim Bradley has some critical needs that could be addressed by one or more of those features? Or maybe you and Jim could discover those needs together?"

"I get it," Mitch said, perking up. "The Best Questions I could ask Jim are open-ended questions that probe for needs corresponding to my strongest features."

"More precisely, you want to probe for needs that correspond to the *benefits* of those features. Because Jim doesn't need product features, of course, he needs the benefits they provide—the things those features can do to help him achieve goals he cares about."

> *"The Best Questions probe for needs of my strongest features."*

Mitch nodded to show that he was familiar with the distinction between features and benefits. Harry wrote the following on a fresh sheet of paper:

Selling Strengths
↓
Benefits
↓
Buyer's Need
↓
Open-Ended Questions

"You've just completed the first step of a questioning process that Action Selling calls *Back-Tracking Benefits*," Harry told him. "To Ask the Best Questions that uncover needs your products or services could help solve, you work backwards from the thing you're selling. First you identify your selling strengths. Then you identify the common benefits of those strengths—what makes them appealing to most customers? Before calling on a customer, you prepare some questions designed to reveal needs for those benefits. During the call you listen carefully for clues that allow you to probe deeper and ask more specific questions about how a product benefit would help this *particular* customer."

"I get it," Mitch said again, taking notes.

*Do you?* Harry thought. *I don't think so.* "Remember," he said, "you just told me that the strengths you've identified aren't exactly unique. If you're like most salespeople, your competitors can offer similar features and benefits. What you need to understand, Mitch, is that almost nobody today has a genuinely unique product to sell. The winner is the salesperson who is most skillful at executing a process. That process involves asking questions that raise the customer's awareness of particular kinds of needs—and how those needs could be satisfied by working together with the salesperson.

> *"The winner is the salesperson who is most skillful at executing a process."*

If this isn't the whole ballgame, it's certainly the first eight innings."

Mitch looked him in the eye. "Okay, Harry. I won't say, 'I get it.' But I'm starting to get it." He held the gaze until Harry nodded his acceptance. "Now, how do I go about it? I mean, I can't just walk into Jim Bradley's office, ask a few general Act 2 questions about his background to build rapport, and then say, 'Jim, I have 99 more questions. Here's Number 1.'"

Harry just smiled and grabbed another sheet of paper. He drew a diagram that looked like this:

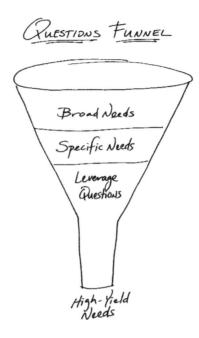

When he finished drawing, Harry said: "Think of questions as investments you make during a sales call, Mitch. If you don't invest wisely, you won't get a return. A few well-planned questions can produce an enormous payoff on your investment. But there's an art to it—a process. Action Selling uses this Questions Funnel to illustrate how it works."

He let Mitch examine the drawing, then continued. "You're absolutely right about 'Here are 99 questions I want to ask.' The customer would throw you out of his office. The same thing would happen if the first question out of your mouth were what Action

Selling calls a Leverage Question. A Leverage Question is one that turns up the emotional heat under a need you've identified. It's the most important question you'll ask—the investment with the biggest payoff—but it isn't the first one you'll ask with regard to any individual need.

"The funnel shows you how to structure your questions about needs related to each product benefit you want to explore," Harry went on. "First you ask a broad question about a need related to the benefit. Then ask a couple of questions to clarify and specify the need. Then you ask a Leverage Question to raise the customer's awareness of how important the need really is.

*"The funnel shows how to structure questions about needs for each product benefit."*

"A Leverage Question urges the customer to recognize—on a personal, emotional level—the full danger or opportunity hiding in this need. What's really in it for Bridgeco if Jim Bradley solves the problem or grasps the opportunity he's talking to you about? Better still, what's in it for Jim personally? What pain will he suffer if he fails to solve the problem? What reward might he get if he does solve it? A good Leverage Question leads the customer to think, 'Holy cow, I've got to *do* something about this!'

"But you have to set the stage for a Leverage Question," Harry concluded. "You need to earn the right to ask one. It's like I told you before: Each good question you ask earns you the right to ask the next question. Each good question helps you 'sell yourself' and build a relationship in which you become a trusted consultant and partner, working *with* the customer toward a solution. I said that questions are investments. *What you're investing in is that relationship!* If you can build it, your competitors will have a very tough time trying to breach it."

Mitch sat still, gazing at some point in space outside Harry's office window. Finally he said, "That's what you mean about the customer's first major buying decision being the most important one, isn't it? Whether to 'buy' the salesperson. It really is enormous."

> *"You need to earn the right to ask a Leverage Question."*

"*Now* you're starting to get it," Harry said softly. *You've finally stepped onto the path to enlightenment*, he thought.

Mitch was quiet for another minute. Then he said, "Okay, how do I do this with Jim Bradley?"

"Start by preparing a few questions for each of the three strengths you've identified," Harry replied. "You may have to improvise based on what you hear from Jim—that's where effective listening comes in. But start with a plan. What do you say we work through an example with one of your three features? Pick one."

"How about 'easiest access to technical support'?"

"All right." Harry drew another Questions Funnel on his pad, with no labels. "You want to start with a broad question that will get Jim thinking and talking about his needs for easy access to technical support. For instance, what problems does he have with tech support for his current system?"

"I'll bet I can guess," Mitch said eagerly. "I know what system he's using."

"That's good. Your experience will help. But you're there to ask and listen, not to guess. No, don't look glum," Harry laughed, noting Mitch's expression. "Here's where educated guessing *does* come in. Action Selling recommends that you 'preface' a broad needs question with something from your own experience that prompts the customer and also shows that you know something about the issue.

*"Preface a broad needs question with something from your own experience."*

"For instance, instead of asking, "Jim, what problems do you run into with tech support?" you might say something like this: "Jim, many prospective customers tell me their biggest headache with technical support is that they can't reach a service rep when they need one. Others feel they simply shouldn't need to call for tech help as often as they do. When your people need technical support for your current system, what do they do?"

Mitch jotted notes furiously. "Yeah, that makes sense," he said. "By framing the question that way, I 'sell myself' as someone familiar with the kinds of issues that arise in companies around tech support. Jim is more willing to talk to me about his problems because he figures maybe I have some expertise that could help him. I earn the right to ask the question while I'm asking it."

"Bravo," Harry said. "Do you want to pick a broad needs question for Bradley?"

"I like the one you just gave me," Mitch said. "I'll preface it the way you suggested, then ask him, 'What do your people currently do when they need technical support?'"

"Fine," Harry said, making a note on his drawing of the

Questions Funnel. "Next you'll ask one or more specific questions, based on his answer to the broad one. If he describes a more or less general problem with tech support, you want to know exactly what that problem looks like to Jim—in *his* situation, in *his* company—and the effects it has on *his* operation. But it's more than just you wanting to know. You also want *him* to think through his own need and its implications. He may never have taken the time to do that. Your questions should help him."

With some coaching from Harry, Mitch settled on two questions to encourage Jim Bradley to paint a more specific picture of his needs: "Can you tell me about the last time your people had trouble getting a question

> *"It's more than you wanting to know. You want him to think through his own need."*

answered by tech support?" And, as a follow-up: "How did that affect their ability to service your customers?"

Harry made more notes on his Questions Funnel. Then he said, "That last question, about the impact on Bridgeco or Jim's department, may turn out to be a Leverage Question on its own. If the effect of second-rate tech support on Jim's operation is so dramatic that the personal consequences to him are glaringly obvious, then it *is* a Leverage Question. But to raise the emotional heat under his need for better tech support, there's still one more question we could ask him."

Mitch grinned like a student one step ahead of the teacher. "When customers aren't getting the service that they expect, how does that impact *you*, Jim?" he said.

Harry responded by turning around his drawing of the Questions Funnel. He had already written that very question at the bottom. His picture looked like this:

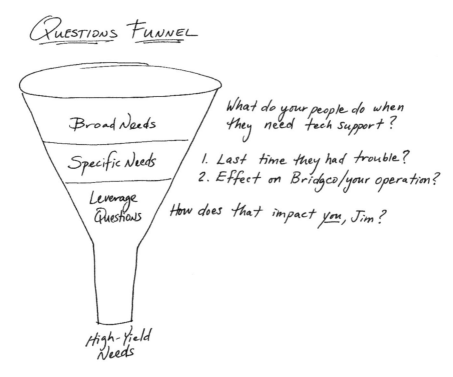

**Questions Funnel**

Broad Needs — What do your people do when they need tech support?

Specific Needs —
1. Last time they had trouble?
2. Effect on Bridgco/your operation?

Leverage Questions — How does that impact you, Jim?

High-Yield Needs

"Go through that same process to plan questions that relate to needs for your other two strongest features," Harry said. "Plan some early Act 2 questions as well, based on what you know about Bridgeco and Jim Bradley's background. Above all, *listen* to what he tells you and react accordingly. You need to plan, but don't hesitate to ditch your plan if the customer leads you in a different direction. Maybe his major problem with his current system doesn't correspond to the three features you picked. Fine. Probe it with the same kinds of questions. How is your product or service able to solve the problems he cares about the most? Never mind the features you're so proud of. When you present a solution to Jim later, you'll have to tell him how you'll solve *his* problem. Let him tell you what it is. Ask him to describe it. Ask him what effects it

## *"Shut up and listen!"*

has on Bridgco and on him personally. For crying out loud, shut up and *listen* to the man!"

Mitch scribbled a final note, then leaned back in his chair. "You haven't told me everything there is to Action Selling, have you, Harry?"

"Not even close. But if you use what I've told you, you're going to have a very different kind of selling experience with Jim Bradley. And then you're going to want to get certified as an Action Selling professional."

Mitch rose and shook Harry's hand. "I have a feeling you're right," he said. "Thanks, Harry. Really. Thanks."

"You owe me five bucks," Harry said. "That guy hit it sideways but he did *not* corkscrew himself into the ground."

# Chapter 5

## MEANWHILE, BACK IN THE CUSTOMER'S HEAD...

*'I think this guy can actually help me.'*

"If Bridgeco intends to grow from $500 million to $1 billion in revenue, I'm sure you'll need to make changes in the way you acquire the products you sell. What concerns do you have about your ability to handle the increased volume?" Mitch asked Jim Bradley.

"We'll have to find efficiencies within our supply chain," Bradley replied. "We certainly don't want to grow without a corresponding reduction in our cost of doing business."

*I can't believe I'm having this level of conversation with a salesperson*, Bradley thought, not for the first time. *I actually think this guy might be able to help us with some real problems.* The 20 minutes he originally allowed for Mitch's call already had stretched to 40, and Bradley was not at all impatient to end the visit. Quite the opposite.

From the start, this had been anything but a typical sales call. *If he's got a product pitch, I haven't heard it*, Bradley thought. He knew he had revealed far more information about Bridgeco—its workings and its plans—than he ordinarily would regard as any of a salesperson's business. *Or anything a salesperson would care about*, his mind added. He tried again to put his finger on what it was about Mitch that made him want to open up. The closest he could come was this: *He doesn't act as if I obviously need what he's selling. He genuinely seems to want to know whether he can help us, and if so, how.*

> **"Mitch genuinely seems to want to know if he can help us."**

Before Mitch walked into Jim Bradley's office, he had done enough research to know that Bridgeco was a $500 million company with about 700 salespeople in 60 branches. It had been easy to learn that Bradley was one of Bridgeco's five majority shareholders and served as vice president of marketing. Mitch also was aware of speculation in the business press that Bridgeco was planning a public stock offer soon. Bradley appreciated the fact that Mitch had prepared for the visit, but there was nothing especially unusual about a salesperson doing a little bit of homework before a call.

No, what *was* unusual was Mitch's desire to understand how Bridgeco operated, what it wanted to achieve, the obstacles it faced, and the problems that might be important to Bradley himself. Bradley had expected a few minutes of chit-chat followed by a product presentation. Faced instead with a listener whose questions showed a sincere interest in him and in his company, he began talking. *And I haven't shut up since*, he thought with some surprise. *What's more, I don't want to shut up. I don't know if this guy has a solution for me, but he's helping me think through some issues I haven't really considered.*

Earlier in the call, Bradley had confirmed that Bridgeco indeed wanted to go public. He acknowledged that each of the five owners had a huge stake in the public offering. The success of that offering

> *"Mitch's desire to understand how we operated was unusual."*

hinged on Bridgeco's ability to show progressive growth in line with an ambitious plan to double its revenue to $1 billion within five years. This growth would come from expansion into global markets. In the course of explaining Bridgeco's workings, Bradley also had turned over some cards he ordinarily would have held closer to his vest when dealing with an unfamiliar salesperson—such as the fact that major buying decisions required the approval of all five stakeholders.

> *Bradley turned over some cards he ordinarily would have held closer to his vest.*

As for Mitch, he had suspected as much, and firmed up his Commitment Objective for the call accordingly: *I want Jim to agree to let me present a proposal to all of the owners.*

Mitch's mind was operating on two levels. On one level there was surprise and delight at how well things were going and a keen awareness that this was unlike any sales call he had ever made. But those feelings were overshadowed by his engagement with what Bradley was telling him. The inside look he was getting into Bridgeco's operations was actually fascinating. As the call progressed, Mitch found that asking open-ended questions had become easy and natural for the simple reason that he *really did* want to understand the issues Bradley faced, and he really had begun to think in terms of solutions he might offer, not just products he might sell. *I came in wanting to act like a consultant. Now I'm thinking like one,* he realized. *I wonder how many other clients I would find this interesting if I just let them tell me what their worlds look like.*

> **"I came in wanting to act like a consultant. Now I'm thinking like one."** | *I wonder how much I'd learn about all kinds of things. I wonder how much more I'd enjoy my job.*

Fortunately, it was Bradley, not Mitch, who got caught woolgathering. "I'm sorry," he said. "What did you ask?"

"We were talking about the need to find efficiencies within your supply chain," Mitch reminded him. "All of my customers want to improve their product-acquisition processes. For some of my customers, the key issue is product cost. Others are most concerned with accuracy, speed and fill rates. I asked what it is about your current procurement methods that will have to improve in order to handle the increase in volume you'll experience as Bridgeco grows."

"What *won't* have to improve?" Bradley laughed. "Speed, accuracy, fill rates—everything involved in our acquisition process will need to be overhauled." *There you go again,* he thought. *That's just what our management team has been wrestling with.*

> ***That's just what our management team has been wrestling with.*** | "If you don't find a good way to handle the overhaul, what will the consequences be?"

Bradley thought that one over for several seconds. "In a word, the consequences would be unacceptable," he said. "Why grow at all if we can't make money doing it?"

"Who is ultimately responsible for finding a solution to the problem?"

"Well, all five of us on the management team will have to put our heads together."

Mitch put a mental checkmark next to his Commitment Objective. *Yes, I want a meeting with the whole management team. But not before I've gathered more ammunition.*

"What do you recommend we do?" Bradley asked.

*Whoa, Jim, you're jumping to Act 6,* Mitch thought, Harry's Action Selling terminology coming to mind with surprising ease. *I'm not ready to sell my product yet, and you're not ready to make a buying decision about it. We're in Act 3 now, and you're still deciding whether to buy me.* "I have some ideas," he answered aloud. "But I'd like to get a clearer picture of the needs a good solution would have to address. Is that okay?"

"Sure," Bradley said. "But let me ask you a question. How do you track your order fulfillment rates?" *You're all over our issues, Mitch,* he thought, *and I like your game, and I wish more salespeople behaved the way you do. But it's time I found out if you've actually got something we can use.*

> *I wish more salespeople behaved the way you do.*

Mitch sensed that the question wasn't a casual one. He remembered how stupid he'd felt when Harry pointed out the folly of his thoughtless answer to Cheryl Gross's question about lead-time. *There's some kind of drop-dead issue here, isn't there, Jim?* he thought. *You're qualifying me. Careful.*

So, without knowing it, Mitch did exactly what Action Selling would have told him to do. He answered Bradley's question with a question: "Tracking performance in our distribution center is a very high priority for my company," he said. "What kind of information do you want to receive?"

"Well, it's not just a matter of your distribution center," Bradley replied. "If our purchasing process is really going to get streamlined, we need access not just to our direct suppliers but to *their* suppliers. Too many problems come up when our people have trouble tracking an order that's stalled somewhere in a vendor's supply chain."

*Jim, I could kiss you,* Mitch thought. *You just helped me 'Backtrack a Benefit' of one of my strongest features.* Resisting the powerful urge to tell Bradley then and there that his company was the best in the industry at ensuring client access to its entire supply chain, Mitch asked: "Tell me about a recent situation when lack of access caused a problem."

Bradley did. Since Mitch knew he had a great solution to this problem he decided to turn up the heat on the need. So he posed his leverage question: "What are the consequences to you and the other owners if problems like that aren't solved before your purchasing volume expands dramatically?"

*Leverage Question: "What are the consequences if problems like that aren't solved?"*

Even before Bradley responded, Mitch could see the realization written in the man's face and knew exactly what Jim was thinking: *Our big pay day, the public placement, won't be what we want it to be. Holy cow, I've got to do something about this!*

On they went, Mitch doing the asking, Bradley doing the talking. The call had lasted more than an hour before Bradley glanced at his watch. *Time to wrap this up*, Mitch thought. *I think I have plenty of ammo.*

"Jim, let me see if I can summarize the major issues that you need a solution to address." Consulting the notes he had taken, Mitch said, "First, since you'll be expanding into international markets as part of your push for revenue growth, you need a supplier with top-notch experience in dealing with the transition into global markets." *Like my company*, he added to himself.

Bradley nodded.

"Second," Mitch continued, "your procurement process has to get streamlined to be faster, more economical, and more responsive. A key to that will be that your people should have easy access to information not just from your direct supplier but also from the whole supply chain.

*"Let me summarize the major issues: Transition into global markets, streamline procurement process and 24/7 technical support."*

"Third, while you're satisfied with your current supplier's technical support, you'll need access to technical support 24/7 so that issues arising from your global expansion can be dealt with before they create problems for your customers." *Thank God my questions here in Act 3 uncovered how happy you are with the tech support you get from your current supplier,* Mitch thought. *If this had come up as an objection later in the sales process, it would have bitten me right on the behind. Now that I know about it, I can not only defuse the potential objection but also use it to my advantage during my custom presentation.*

Bradley was already nodding again when Mitch asked, "Do I have all that right?"

"Yes, that's a good summary." *You weren't just pretending to pay attention while I did all the talking, were you,* he thought.

Mitch smiled. "We can help you, Jim. In fact, as you grow to a billion-dollar company, we'll be a perfect match for Bridgeco. Here's what I'd like to suggest as a next step. If you would arrange the meeting, I'll come back and present a proposal to you and the others on your management team. I'll explain exactly how my company would address the needs you've described, and I'll answer any questions that you or the others have. How does that sound?"

*Well, I'd like to know what your outfit could do for us, and I think the rest of the team would too,* Bradley thought. *Besides, I wouldn't mind having you as my primary contact for a supplier.* "That sounds good, Mitch," he said. "How about next Wednesday at 2 o'clock? The management team has a regular meeting at one, and I think I can persuade everyone to extend it to hear your proposal."

"That would work for me," Mitch thought. *I'll make it work,* he thought.

"Fine. I'll confirm our meeting by email, but barring something drastic that comes up, we'll see you next Wednesday. And I'll look forward to it," Bradley said, rising to shake hands.

"Me too, Jim. We'll make good use of our time together." *In fact, I'll bet I can give your team the most on-target proposal they've ever heard.*

# Epilogue

*Learning a new game*

B y the sixth hole, Harry knew he was doomed. Mitch was on fire—striping it down the fairways, hitting shots onto greens that knocked the flags down, and putting like a demon.

"Going to win back the money I took from you the last time we played, is that it?" Harry asked.

"That's the plan," Mitch said happily, after his approach shot left him with a five-foot birdie putt.

"Ungrateful dog, aren't you."

"Harry, I am the most grateful dog you ever knew. But I'm still going to take your money. You can afford it. And now I know why you can afford it, since I understand your secret weapon."

*You think you understand Action Selling already?* Harry thought. *That's peculiar, since I'm still learning and improving at it. Guess I can't take off my mentor hat just yet.*

When Mitch had called to invite Harry to play golf again, his excitement was so great that Harry had to hold the phone away from his ear. "Unbelievable!" Mitch kept shouting. "Harry, the difference was unbelievable!"

Mitch had just landed the Bridgeco account. ("Suddenly I'm a rainmaker around here!") He talked as if Harry couldn't possibly appreciate the remarkableness of his initial call on Jim Bradley or of his triumphant presentation to Bridgeco's management team. He kept groping for words to describe the experience.

"It was like no call I ever made!" Mitch had exclaimed. "The whole tone of it was different."

> ## "It was like no call I ever made!"

"I imagine so, if you were listening to Bradley's voice instead of your own," Harry replied dryly.

Mitch laughed. "Yeah, but it went way beyond that. It was amazing how Bradley opened up when I started asking him the Best Questions. No client has ever talked to me that frankly or told me so much about his business. I felt like a management consultant. Heck, I started to *think* like a consultant. Bradley liked me and trusted me. And I felt like I deserved his trust. It was as if—I don't know, as if the whole focus was on what I could do to help solve his problems

> ## "No client has ever talked to me that frankly."

instead of on what products I could sell him.

"And you know what?" Mitch continued. "The same feeling carried over even when I made my presentation to the management team—even when I *was* talking about my products. It wasn't about 'Here's my stuff.' It was about, 'Here's your situation, here's what we all know your problems are, and here's how I can help.' A big part of it was that Bradley and I had already agreed on Bridgeco's needs, and he had 'bought me,' and he obviously had helped 'sell me' to the others before I even walked into the meeting. But there was more to it. I felt like I was on *their* side—not just selling something, but helping them solve real problems and meet real needs. I had so much information about Bridgeco that I felt almost like an insider."

"You found Bridgeco more interesting than a typical client company, did you?" Harry asked.

"Absolutely! That's just it, Harry, my whole job was more interesting. I really got caught up in learning about Bridgeco and..." Mitch broke off and laughed. "Sorry, I keep forgetting that you already know what a difference Action Selling makes."

That was when Mitch ended the phone conversation by inviting Harry to play another round of golf. *And he's already four up. I'm afraid to press him; I'd just lose more money*, Harry

## "My job is more interesting."

thought as they walked to the seventh tee. *I'm happy for you, Mitch. But you're not finished learning. Not by a long shot.*

"Remember what I said about Act 9 of Action Selling—Replay the Call?" he asked. "Do you want to walk through it with me?"

"Sure," Mitch said.

"All right, what was your Commitment Objective going into the call on Jim Bradley? And did you have to change it?"

Mitch shook his head. "Thanks to you, I went in with the right Commitment Objective. Instead of trying to 'sell' him, I used the time to sell myself by asking questions. My Commitment Objective was for him to agree to let me come back and make a presentation

> **"Instead of trying to 'sell' him, I used the time to sell myself by asking questions."**

to everyone involved in the buying decision—after I gathered enough ammunition to make a *good* presentation, I mean. I confirmed that objective during the call, and I didn't change it."

"Good," Harry said. *And my Commitment Objective for this conversation, Mitch, is to get you to agree that you aren't finished learning about Action Selling. You're not certified yet.* "So in the initial call, you wanted to concentrate on Acts 2, 3 and 4—People Skills, Ask the Best Questions, and Agree on Needs. I take it things went well, but what problems did you run into?"

"No problems at all," Mitch said. "Things went amazingly well. I've never felt so much in control of a call—which is ironic, because Bradley did 90 percent of the talking. You know, Harry, I actually have a lot of insight into needs and issues like Bridgeco's—I see enough of them. But when I try to demonstrate what I know by talking, clients don't want to hear it. I was able to show Bradley that I was knowledgeable just by the questions I asked and the way I phrased them. Wow, did that make a difference!

> **"I've never felt so much in control of a call—Bradley did 90 percent of the talking."**

"Oh, and you'll like this, Harry: A couple of times he asked me questions that were like big, fat invitations for me to start a product spiel. But I remembered what you said about keeping the customer's buying decisions in the right order and not jumping ahead to Act 6. So I kept on asking questions to gather information. At one point, I almost had to bite my tongue to keep from telling him all about our order-tracking system. You see, he asked me a question that felt kind of odd, as if it were strangely significant. And instead of answering right away..."

"You answered his question with a question of your own?" Harry interrupted.

"Yes. How'd you know?"

"You said I'd like this part. Answering a question with a question is exactly what Action Selling recommends when a customer raises an issue that you suspect might be a landmine. Instead of stepping on the mine with a thoughtless answer, you need to probe for understanding of the real issue behind the customer's question. So you should ask a clarifying question of your own. Which is what you did—and I know that because if you hadn't, you wouldn't be this happy. Good for you, Mitch."

Mitch grinned broadly, then winked at Harry as he dropped a 20-foot putt. "Yeah, I think I executed it really well," he said. "And since I asked the Best Questions—the Very Best Questions," he added, twirling his putter in exaggerated self-satisfaction, "I also uncovered an objection about technical support that would have come back at me for sure in my presentation if I weren't prepared for it. Since I'm now an Action Selling ace, of course, I anticipated it and knocked it right in the hole." He took a mock swing with the putter to illustrate.

*I know you're half-kidding,* Harry thought, *but I hope you real-*

*ize how much you have yet to learn. Let's find out.* "Mitch, I'm glad that the little I told you about Action Selling helped you land the Bridgeco account. Now, what's your plan to build on that success?"

## I hope you realize how much you have yet to learn.

Surprised that Harry would even ask, Mitch turned to answer, then hesitated. *So that guy at your club didn't literally screw himself into the ground, eh, Harry? You're not the only one who can yank somebody's chain.* "Don't worry about me, Buddy," he said, as if he hadn't a care in the world. "Now that I know how to make a real, professional sales call and a real product presentation, I'll be just fine."

"Oh?" Harry said, taken aback. "You think you'll be just fine with what you know now?"

"Sure. Look what I just did at Bridgeco. What else could I need?"

"Has it been your experience that old habits are that easy to break?" Harry asked, getting exasperated. "You do something differently one time, and, bang, your behavior changes for good?"

"Yep," Mitch said.

Harry goggled at him. "That was a close-ended question," Mitch added.

Just as it began to dawn on Harry that he was being had, Mitch lost control and doubled over laughing. For half a minute he howled, unable to speak.

"You should have seen the look on your face, Harry," he gasped, when he was able to talk again. "Gee, do you think I should get trained and certified in Action Selling? Did you figure it might be tough to get me to realize it and agree to it? Because I'm, like, 'Duh!'" He started laughing again.

Harry turned away, smiling, and hit a 7-iron into the 10th green. "So," he said, "I take it you're already highly motivated to learn more about Action Selling?"

"After you told me that *you're* still working on improving your skills? Harry, do you really think I'd have let you get off this course today *without* telling me how to get trained and certified? I'd have *made* you tell me! I did great at Bridgeco, working with what you gave me. It was the best sales experience I ever had. But I know I got lucky, too. Every client won't be as receptive as Jim Bradley was, and I'll bet Action Selling has plenty more to tell me about how to get past the rough spots."

"Yes, it does," Harry said. "And don't forget that there are nine Acts in the system. You and I concentrated on Asking the Best Questions in Acts 2 and 3—and you have a lot more to learn about that, never mind the other seven Acts. But, Mitch, you need to know that Action Selling certification isn't just a piece of paper somebody hands you because you go to a seminar. It takes time and work."

Mitch laughed again. "My whole career takes time and work. These past few years, I've learned what it's like to work hard without getting anywhere. Now that I know the difference Action Selling can make, even for a novice like me, I'd be an idiot if I didn't want to become

> *"Action Selling certification isn't just a piece of paper."*

a master. No, Harry, the question isn't whether I'll agree to do whatever it takes to get certified. The question is, how can I thank you for saving my career?"

When Mitch finished speaking he wasn't smiling anymore. He stepped directly in front of Harry and looked him in the eyes, as if to say: *I'm serious. How can I thank you?*

Harry regarded him thoughtfully. Then he stepped around Mitch, as if considering the question, and plum-bobbed a difficult putt that would break sharply to the right. Finally he addressed the ball. "That's easy," he said. "You can pay me my five bucks. Because that guy did *not* screw himself into the ground."

Harry sank his putt.

# ORDER MORE BOOKS!

  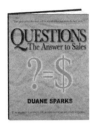

## TO ORDER BOOKS:

- Call (800) 232-3485
- www.ActionSelling.com
- Fax (763) 473-0109
- Mail to The Sales Board

| | |
|---|---|
| $19.95 | Retail |
| 5.00 | Discount |
| $14.95 | Reader Price |

---

### BOOK ORDER FORM

| QUANTITY | BOOK |
|---|---|
| ☐ | Action Selling |
| ☐ | Selling Your Price |
| ☐ | Questions: The Answer to Sales |

**SHIPPING AND HANDLING**
$3.95 per US order
Can/Int'l actual cost
Payable in US funds

---

## BILL MY CREDIT CARD

**THE SALES BOARD**
15200 25ᵀᴴ AVE. N.
PLYMOUTH, MN 55447

Card# _____ Exp. _____

DISC _____ VISA_____ MC _____ AMEX_____

Signature _____

---

Bill to _____

Address _____

City _____ ST _____ Zip _____

Daytime phone _____

Ship to _____

Address _____

City _____ ST _____ Zip _____

# of Books _____

Price $ 14.95_____

Total $_____

MN Sales Tax $_____

Ship/Handling $ 3.95_____

Total Due $_____

---

Please allow 5-7 days for US Delivery. Can/Int'l orders please allow 10 days.
**This offer is subject to change without notice**

# GET TRAINED AND CERTIFIED AS AN
## *ACTION SELLING* PROFESSIONAL!

Want to learn more about how Action Selling can help your organization realize its full sales potential? For information about training and certification for yourself or your salespeople, contact The Sales Board.

Founded in 1990, The Sales Board has boosted the performance of more than 2,500 companies and 200,000 salespeople worldwide in virtually every industry. Action Selling provides a systematic approach to managing and conducting the entire sales process. Our complete training program provides all the necessary tools for students and instructors. Training is customized specifically for each organization's selling situation and even for individual salespeople.

Studies document that veteran salespeople who become Action Selling Certified improve their sales performance by an annual average of 16 percent. As for rookie salespeople, there is no finer system to start them off on the right foot and make them productive immediately.

Students participate in a highly interactive two-day training session facilitated by our talented trainers or by their own Action Selling Certified managers. Students then take part in Skill Drills to refine and reinforce their new skills in the field. Accountability is built into the process with management reinforcement, plus an assessment and certification system.

To learn more about the complete Action Selling training and certification system, please contact us or visit our Web site:

**The Sales Board**
**(800) 232-3485**
**info@thesalesboard.com**
**www.TheSalesBoard.com**

# ABOUT THE AUTHOR

Duane Sparks is chairman and founder of The Sales Board, a Minneapolis-based company that has trained and certified more than 200,000 salespeople in the system and the skills of Action Selling. He is the author of the Best Selling books: *Action Selling, How to sell like a professional even if you think you are one* and *Selling Your Price, How to escape the race to the bargain basement.*

In a 30-year career as a salesperson and sales manager, Duane has sold products ranging from office equipment to insurance. He was the top salesperson at every company he ever worked for. He developed Action Selling while owner of one of the largest computer marketers in the United States. Even in the roaring computer business of the 1980s, his company grew six times faster than the industry norm, differentiating itself not by the products it offered but by the way it sold them. Duane founded The Sales Board in 1990 to teach the skills of Action Selling to others.